Sinkholes

ANN O. SQUIRE

Children's Press®
An Imprint of Scholastic Inc.

Content Consultant

William Barnart, PhD
Assistant Professor
Department of Earth and Environmental Sciences
University of Iowa
Iowa City, Iowa

Library of Congress Cataloging-in-Publication Data

Squire, Ann O., author.
 Sinkholes / by Ann O. Squire.
    pages cm. — (A true book)
Summary: "Learn all about sinkholes, from how they are formed to how they can affect people around the world"— Provided by publisher.
 Includes bibliographical references and index.
 ISBN 978-0-531-22296-6 (library binding : alk. paper) — ISBN 978-0-531-22512-7 (pbk. : alk. paper)
1. Sinkholes—Juvenile literature. I. Title. II. Series: True book.
 GB609.2.S68 2016
 551.44'7—dc23   2015020021

All rights reserved. Published in 2016 by Children's Press, an imprint of Scholastic Inc.
Printed in China 62
SCHOLASTIC, CHILDREN'S PRESS, A TRUE BOOK™, and associated logos are trademarks and/or registered trademarks of Scholastic Inc.
1 2 3 4 5 6 7 8 9 10 R 25 24 23 22 21 20 19 18 17 16

Front cover: A giant sinkhole in Guatelmala City, Guatelmala, in 2007
Back cover: A fire truck caught in a sinkhole

Find the Truth!

Everything you are about to read is true *except* for one of the sentences on this page.

Which one is **TRUE**?

T or F   Sinkholes can sometimes appear suddenly and without warning.

T or F   Sinkholes develop where the underlying rock is very hard.

Find the answers in this book.

3

Contents

THE **BIG** TRUTH!

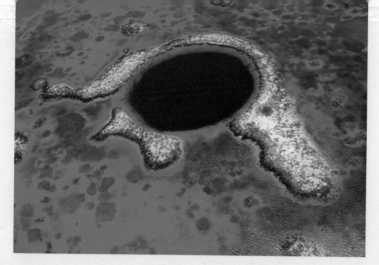

Sinkholes sometimes occur underwater.

Plants and animals live at the bottom of China's Heavenly Pit.

CHAPTER 1

What on Earth?

It was late in the evening on February 28, 2013. Jeremy Bush and his wife, Rachel, were cleaning up after dinner in their Florida home. Jeremy's older brother, 37-year-old Jeff, had gone to bed earlier. He was staying in a bedroom that had once belonged to the Bushes' daughter, Hannah. As Jeremy and Rachel chatted in the kitchen, they were startled by a huge crash and a scream coming from the direction of the bedroom.

← The sinkhole at the Bush home was about 20 feet (6 meters) across.

A Shocking Sight

Jeremy ran to Jeff's bedroom and flung open the door. What he saw was astonishing. Pictures were still hanging on the bedroom walls, but the rest of the room—the floor, the bed, the dresser, and even Jeff himself—had vanished. In its place was a gigantic hole full of dirt. Jeremy thought he could see the corner of the bed poking up through the rubble, but everything else was gone.

While the Bushes' home looked normal from the outside, there was a big problem going on below the surface.

Rescue workers did everything they could to save Jeff Bush, but it was too late.

Rescue Attempt

Jeremy called out to Jeff. Then he jumped into the hole and began digging, trying to find his brother. But as he worked, the hole grew larger. More soil and **debris** from around the edges crumbled inside. In the kitchen, Rachel dialed 911 and reported the emergency. Before long, rescue crews arrived at the house. They pulled Jeremy from the rapidly growing hole, but they could not find Jeff.

The Bushes' entire home had to be torn down due to the sinkhole beneath it.

A Sad Conclusion

Authorities concluded that it was too dangerous for anyone to enter the home. Instead, they attached a camera to a long pole and stuck it through the bedroom window. There was no sign of Jeff or the furniture that had fallen into the hole. In the next few days, it became clear that several neighboring houses were also at risk. Along with the Bushes' house, they were **condemned** and torn down. Jeff Bush's body was never found.

Are You at Risk?

Stories of people being killed in sinkholes are terrifying. But what are the real risks? The chances of falling into a sinkhole are very small. Still, it pays to be prepared. Find out whether the area where you live is prone to sinkholes. You can check maps on the U.S. Geological Survey Web site. Be on the alert for signs of developing sinkholes. These signs can include low spots in the ground, tilted fences, or cracks in sidewalks. Staying alert could save your life!

A 2015 sinkhole in Naples, Italy, affected hundreds of people living nearby.

CHAPTER 2

Holes in the Ground

The Bushes were victims of a sinkhole, a depression or hole in the ground that can form either gradually or very suddenly. Some sinkholes occur naturally, while others are caused or made worse by human activities. Sometimes a sinkhole doesn't look very dramatic at all. It may just seem like a low spot in the ground. But beneath every sinkhole are layers of activity.

The same process that causes sinkholes to form can also result in underground caverns.

13

How Sinkholes Form

The top layer of Earth, or **overburden**, is made of soil. Beneath the soil is a rocky layer called **bedrock**. In some parts of the world, bedrock is made of very hard rock, such as granite. In others, it is formed from a softer type of rock, such as limestone or gypsum. Sinkholes are most likely to form in areas where the bedrock is soft and able to dissolve in water. These areas are known as **karst** terrain.

Overburden

Bedrock

The overburden can be anywhere from a few inches to many feet deep.

Streams are a major source of the acidic water that makes its way underground to the bedrock.

Limestone or similar soft rocks are one part of the recipe for a sinkhole. The other is water. Rainwater and water from streams and **irrigation** systems absorb carbon dioxide from the air. This turns the water into an **acid**. As it seeps underground, the acidic water starts to dissolve the soft rock. Pathways and channels begin to form in the rock. Over time, these grow larger and larger. Soon there are air-filled pockets in the bedrock.

Some sinkholes form very slowly and do not cause problems for people.

Sinking Soil

If the soil that makes up the top layer is loose and sandy, it begins to trickle down into the empty spaces in the bedrock. This movement of soil gradually forms a bowl-shaped sinkhole on the surface. If the underground spaces are small, the sandy soil may fill them up. The sinkhole's growth may seem to stop. But as water seeps deeper down through the soil and dissolves more bedrock, the sinkhole gradually deepens.

Sinkhole Ponds

In some cases, the tiny cracks and openings at the bottom of a sinkhole can become plugged with soil. Water can no longer flow to deeper layers. Over time, rainwater collects in the hole, and a pond is formed. Sinkholes that appear gradually like this are called cover-subsidence, or **dissolution**, sinkholes. They are usually not dangerous.

This beautiful pond in Arizona was formed from a sinkhole.

Cover-Collapse Sinkholes

The other kind of sinkhole appears suddenly and often without any warning signs. These sinkholes are extremely dangerous. They begin in the same way as dissolution sinkholes, with the erosion of bedrock by water. The difference lies in the type of soil that covers the bedrock. Cover-collapse sinkholes occur where the soil contains clay, which is thick and sticks together like glue.

The sudden appearance of a cover-collapse sinkhole can be very dangerous if it occurs on a roadway.

Bedrock can break down over time, leaving behind an underground cavern.

Water flows into cracks in the bedrock.

Caverns grow.

The soil collapses into sinkholes.

No Warning

As pockets form in the bedrock, some soil falls into those spaces. An empty space starts to form in the soil itself. If the topmost soil contains enough clay, it sticks together and forms a "bridge" over the growing space. From the surface, there is no sign of what is going on below. When the underground space gets large enough, or rain soaks the soil, or a heavy weight is applied, the ground collapses without warning.

Sinkholes in the Dead Sea

Is the Dead Sea dying? Many environmental experts believe that it is. They point to the many sinkholes in the area as proof.

The Dead Sea, which lies between the countries of Israel and Jordan, is Earth's lowest point on land. It lies 1,407 feet (429 m) below sea level. The sea gets its water from the Jordan River, but in recent years much of that water has

been diverted for other uses. With less water coming in, the Dead Sea is shrinking. Salt deposits in the sea's bedrock are flushed out by rainwater and groundwater, creating thousands of sinkholes along the shoreline. New holes open up every day, posing a real danger to residents of the area.

Israel and Jordan have agreed to work together to save the Dead Sea by increasing the amount of water that flows into it. Water from a desalination plant will be pumped back into the sea. A pipeline bringing more water from the Red Sea will also be constructed. Nothing can be done about the sinkholes that already exist. However, if the Dead Sea recovers, experts hope that fewer new holes will form.

CHAPTER 3

Natural and Unnatural Causes

Wherever you find the combination of dissolvable bedrock and water seeping down through the ground, it is possible that sinkholes will develop. These natural causes cannot be avoided. However, many sinkholes are not natural. They are either caused or made worse by human activities. Careless actions by people are responsible for some of the worst sinkholes on Earth today.

 Central Florida has so many sinkholes that it is sometimes called "Sinkhole Alley."

In expanding neighborhoods, dozens of houses are often built all at once.

Too Much Building

As Earth's population increases, cities and towns grow larger and spread out. With more people needing a place to live, builders look for new areas to put up homes and apartments. More and more natural land is developed for use by people. If these areas are already at risk for sinkholes, the results can sometimes be disastrous.

Florida is a good example of this growing problem. The entire state's bedrock is the type of soft, dissolvable rock where sinkholes often form. There are at least 15,000 known sinkholes in Florida. Most are located near the center of the state, but very few areas are safe from possible sinkholes.

Florida suffered about 300 cave-ins between 2010 and 2014.

A Growing Threat

In 1970, nearly 7 million people called Florida home. By 2014, the state's population had grown to nearly 20 million. New homes are being built everywhere. It is possible to test for developing sinkholes before building. The tests are expensive, however. Most builders do not do them. Construction, blasting, and extra weight on the ground can all trigger a sinkhole collapse. As Florida's population grows, the state has greater chances of sinkhole disasters.

Many new homes have been constructed in Florida over the past several decades.

The 1981 Winter Park sinkhole covered a wide area of land.

Not Enough Water

Sinkholes can also form when water levels are low because of **drought**. Low water levels may have triggered one of Florida's worst sinkholes ever. One evening in 1981, a large sinkhole suddenly opened in the town of Winter Park. Soon, trees and a house had fallen into the hole. Over the next few days, the hole got larger, swallowing five cars, a swimming pool, and part of a street.

Pumice and other materials from Pacaya volcano have helped create sinkholes in Guatemala City.

Too Much Water

Too much water flooding the ground can also result in a sinkhole. A tropical storm and a burst sewer pipe were the likely causes of one dramatic sinkhole in the center of Guatemala City in Central America. The city is built atop a layer of loose volcanic rock called pumice. This rock is easily **eroded** and washed away by flowing water.

The giant sinkhole opened up suddenly in May 2010. It measured 65 feet (20 m) across by 300 feet (91 m) deep. Electricity poles and a three-story house fell in. The hundreds of people in the surrounding neighborhood were fearful that the sinkhole would grow and engulf their homes as well. Scientists warn that overloaded sewers combined with the loose rock beneath the city could lead to many more sinkholes in Guatemala City.

The 2010 sinkhole in Guatemala City was deep enough that a 30-story building could have fit inside it.

Salt Mine Sinkhole

Mining is another activity that can cause sinkholes. Residents of Bayou Corne, Louisiana, blame a local salt mine for a sinkhole that opened up in 2012. Salt is mined by forcing water underground to dissolve it. The resulting salty water is pumped out. This leaves a hollow cavity underground. In 1982, a mining company began using this process on a large salt deposit beneath Bayou Corne.

Timeline of Major Modern Sinkholes

1981

A sinkhole in Winter Park, Florida, swallows a house, five cars, a swimming pool, and part of a street.

May 2010

A sinkhole measuring 65 feet (20 m) across opens in Guatemala City, Guatemala.

Disaster in the Bayou

Over the next 30 years, millions of pounds of salt were removed. An empty cavern formed underground. No one knew that one wall of this cavern was dangerously close to underground deposits of oil and natural gas. In August 2012, the side of the cavern collapsed. As mud, swamp water, and trees were sucked into the sinkhole, the underground gas was released and bubbled to the surface.

2012
The Bayou Corne sinkhole opens near a salt mine in Louisiana.

February 28, 2013
A sinkhole opens up beneath the Bush family home in Florida.

Rising water from the sinkhole in Bayou Corne has brought floods to the town.

A Ghost Town

When it first appeared, the Bayou Corne sinkhole measured about 325 feet (99 m) across. More than a year later, it had grown to cover an area the size of 20 football fields. It is still growing today. Residents of the town fear for their safety, both from the growing sinkhole and from the oil and gas fumes coming from underground. Many families have moved away. Bayou Corne is beginning to look like a ghost town.

Repairing Sinkholes

Once a sinkhole has formed, can it be fixed? Is it possible to fill it in? The method used to repair a sinkhole is determined by the hole's size and location. If the hole is in a remote area, authorities may decide to leave it alone. Sinkholes in urban areas are sometimes filled in with concrete or a mixture of sand and cement. The residents of Winter Park, Florida, decided to turn their giant sinkhole into a lake. It is named Lake Rose, in honor of a resident whose house fell into the sinkhole when it opened up in 1981.

In Bayou Corne, workers try to stop the sinkhole from spreading by building walls of dirt.

Orihuela del Tremedal in northeastern Spain is particularly prone to sinkholes.

Amazing Sinkholes Around the World

In addition to Florida and Louisiana, sinkholes are found in many other places around the globe. An area in northeastern Spain is built on top of gypsum, a rock that is even softer than limestone. Sinkholes are very common there. In some towns, the buildings are cracked and tilted because of the unstable ground beneath them.

Many of Spain's sinkholes occur in places near the Ebro River.

Farm Trouble

Farming is a common activity in this part of Spain. This can make the sinkhole problem even worse. Underground caverns form as farmers pump water to irrigate their crops. This makes the ground more likely to collapse under the weight of heavy machinery or even people working in the fields. Spanish farmers sometimes carry long poles across their shoulders to catch themselves from falling into a sinkhole if one opens up.

Farmers in northern Spain must keep a watchful eye for signs of sinkholes.

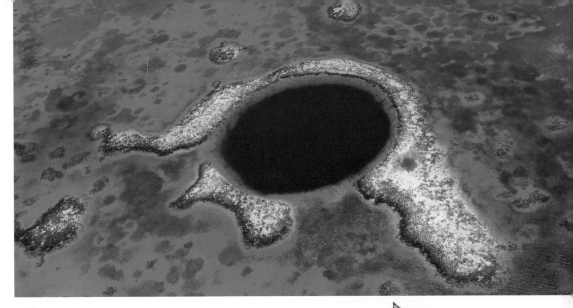

The Great Blue Hole is a popular destination for scuba divers.

The Great Blue Hole

Not all sinkholes are found on land. The Great Blue Hole is located 60 miles (96.5 kilometers) off the coast of Belize. It is a giant underwater sinkhole measuring 984 feet (300 m) across by 410 feet (125 m) deep. Scientists believe that it formed many thousands of years ago, when sea levels were much lower. As sea levels rose, water flooded in and filled the hole.

Sun shines down to the floor of the Heavenly Pit through the sinkhole's opening above.

China's Heavenly Pit

One of the world's largest sinkholes is found in China. Known as the Heavenly Pit, it measures 2,053 feet (626 m) long, 1,761 feet (537 m) wide, and 2,171 feet (662 m) deep. There, visitors can descend steep stone steps deep into the earth, to the bottom of the sinkhole. Lush plants cover the floor of the pit, and an underground river flows through the stone caverns.

Parachuting the Pit

In 2008, three adventurous men decided to parachute into the Heavenly Pit. It was a dangerous plan. The walls of the sinkhole are rocky. The bottom of the pit also contains sharp rocks and a swiftly flowing river. If the men opened their parachutes at the wrong time, landed in the wrong place, or hit the walls on the way down, they could have been injured or killed. Fortunately, the jump was successful.

The Heavenly Pit is locally called Xiaozhai Tiankeng.

CHAPTER 5

Sinkhole Signs

Is it possible to predict where a dangerous sinkhole might occur? Not all sinkholes come with warning signs. However, there are sometimes clues that something is happening underground. Bowl-shaped depressions or ponds that form unexpectedly can indicate a shift of soil. Other signs are cracked or tilted structures and doors that won't shut properly.

Some sinkholes can be found in clusters.

By attaching a pod of sensors to the bottom of an airplane, scientists can scan an area for signs of sinkhole formation.

Using Radar

Scientists are working on new technology that will allow them to predict where sinkholes might develop. Using an airplane with sophisticated radar equipment, they fly over possible sinkhole areas and capture images of the ground. Repeated flights let them compare the radar images over time. This makes it possible to detect very small movements in Earth's crust that can signal a developing sinkhole.

Radar images of the Bayou Corne area showed that the ground had shifted more than 10 inches (25.4 centimeters) in the months before the sinkhole opened. Scientists did not know at the time that this was an early warning of sinkholes. The things they have learned by analyzing images of Bayou Corne and other sinkholes will help them pinpoint threatened areas and give people a chance to evacuate before future disasters strike. ★

Radar images help scientists track the growth of the Bayou Corne sinkhole.

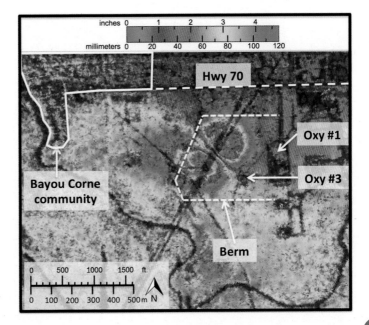

Number of sinkholes that have appeared in Florida since 2010: Approximately 300

Size of Egypt's Qattara Depression, the world's largest natural sinkhole: 50 miles (80.5 km) wide by 75 miles (121 km) long

Cubic yards of soil swallowed by Florida's Winter Park sinkhole: 250,000

Percent of Earth's population living in areas prone to sinkhole development: 25

Percent of the United States where sinkholes could occur: 20

Volume of China's Heavenly Pit: 4,214,770,000 cubic feet (119,349,000 cubic meters)

Number of different plant species that grow in the Heavenly Pit: 1,285

Did you find the truth?

T Sinkholes can sometimes appear suddenly and without warning.

F Sinkholes develop where the underlying rock is very hard.

Resources

Books

Kopp, Megan. *Sinkholes*. New York: AV2 by Weigl, 2013.

Orr, Tamra B. *Studying Sinkholes*. Ann Arbor, MI: Cherry Lake Publishing, 2015.

Important Words

acid (AS-id) — a substance that usually dissolves in water and has a sour taste

bedrock (BED-rahk) — the solid layer of rock under the soil

condemned (kuhn-DEMD) — declared to be unsafe

debris (duh-BREE) — the pieces of something that has been broken or destroyed

desalination (dih-sal-uh-NAY-shun) — the process of removing salt from water

dissolution (dis-uh-LOO-shuhn) — the process of disappearing when mixed with liquid

drought (DOUT) — a long period without rain

eroded (i-RODE-id) — worn away gradually by water or wind

irrigation (ir-uh-GAY-shun) — the process of supplying water to crops by artificial means, such as channels or pipes

karst (KARST) — an area of limestone terrain characterized by sinks, ravines, and underground streams

overburden (OH-vur-bur-duhn) — the layers of soil above bedrock

Index

Page numbers in **bold** indicate illustrations.

About the Author

Ann O. Squire is a psychologist and an animal behaviorist. Before becoming a writer, she studied the behavior of rats, tropical fish in the Caribbean, and electric fish from central Africa. Her favorite part of being a writer is the chance to learn as much as she can about all sorts of topics. In addition to the *Extreme Earth* books, Dr. Squire has written about many different animals, from lemmings to leopards and cicadas to cheetahs. She lives in Long Island City, New York.